SUBTRACTING

FIRST MATH

By Brenda McHale

Published in 2022 by
KidHaven Publishing, an Imprint of Greenhaven Publishing, LLC
29 East 21st Street
New York, NY 10010

Edited by: Robin Twiddy
Designed by: Lydia Wiliams

Cataloging-in-Publication Data

Names: McHale, Brenda.
Title: Subtracting / Brenda McHale.
Description: New York : KidHaven Publishing, 2022. | Series: First math |
Identifiers: ISBN 9781534538924 (pbk.) | ISBN 9781534538948 (library bound) | ISBN 9781534538931 (6 pack) | ISBN 9781534538955 (ebook)
Subjects: LCSH: Subtraction--Juvenile literature. | Arithmetic--Juvenile literature.
Classification: LCC QA115.M343 2022 | DDC 513.2'12--dc23

Printed in the United States of America

CPSIA compliance information: Batch #BSKH22: For further information contact Greenhaven Publishing LLC, New York, New York at 1-844-317-7404.

Please visit our website, www.greenhavenpublishing.com. For a free color catalog of all our high-quality books, call toll free 1-844-317-7404 or fax 1-844-317-7405.

PHOTO CREDITS

Front cover – Veronica Louro. 4 – Ipek Morel. 5 – Tim UR. 6 & 7 – Yuganov Konstantin. 8 – wavebreakmedia, BlueRingMedia. 9 – Ignasi Soler. 12 & 13 – Barbol. 14 & 15 – Peter Vanco, Stock Up, pogonici, Mauro Rodrigues, vsop, Irina Rogova. 16 – IhorL, Oliver Hoffmann, Candus Camera, gresei, oodonwhite, Radu Bercan. 17 – AlohaHawaii. 18 – Happy monkey, Tony Campbell, sekhmister, Cat'chy Images. 19 – LightField Studios, Luis Molinero. 20 – stockphoto-graf, Olga Popova. 21 – Monkey Business Images. 22 – koosen. 23 – Nattika, KirillSaparkin, Tarasyuk Igor, suns07butterfly, Super Prin. 24 – myboys.me.

Images are courtesy of Shutterstock.com. With thanks to Getty Images, Thinkstock Photo, and iStockphoto.

CONTENTS

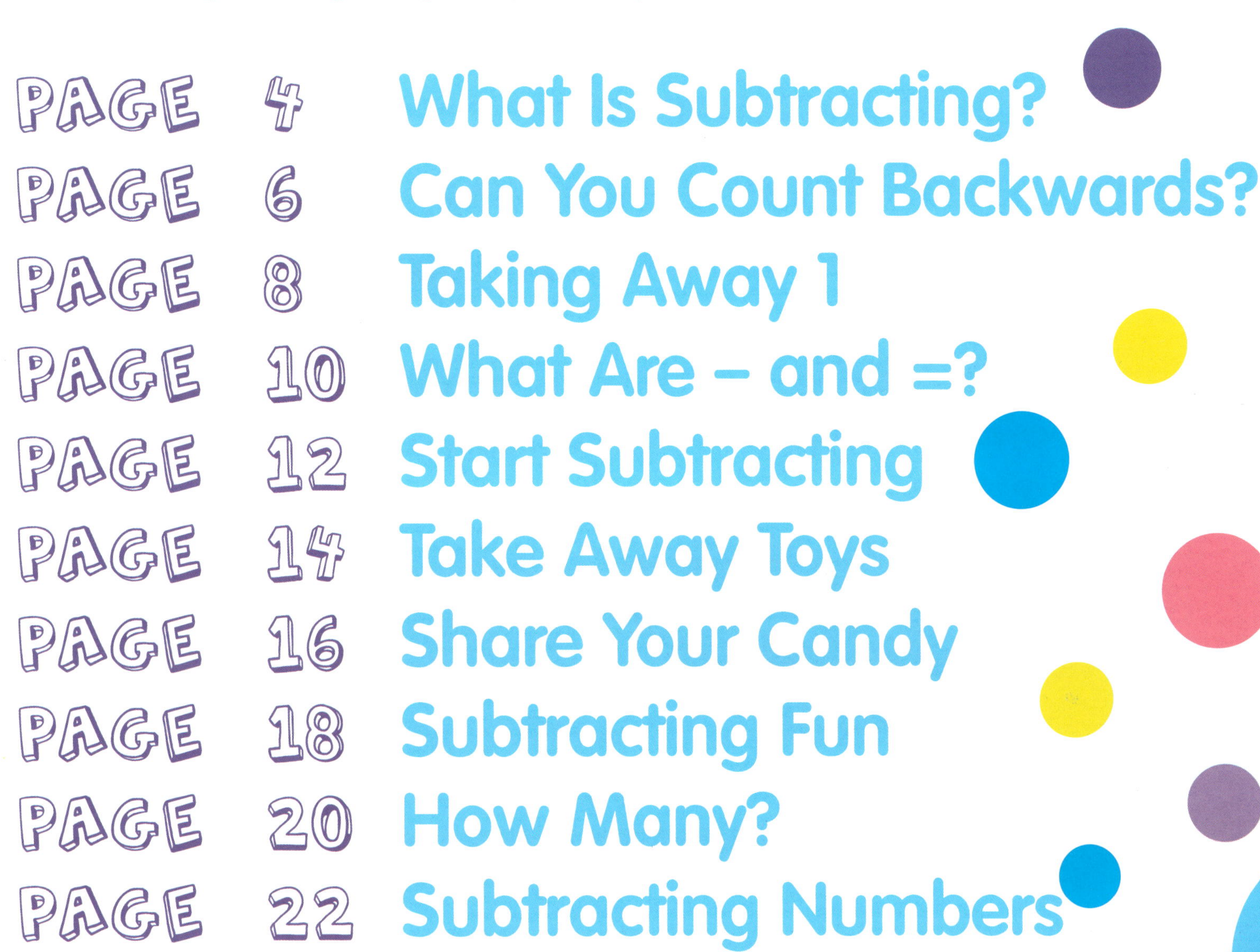

WHAT IS SUBTRACTING?

There are only 3 eggs left in the box.

Subtracting means taking things away.

The small bunch of grapes has fewer grapes than the big bunch.

Fewer means there are not as many.

CAN YOU COUNT BACKWARDS?

Can you count backwards before blastoff?

When space rockets launch, people count backwards to get ready for blastoff.

Start with 10, then 9. When you get to 1, the rocket is ready to launch.

TAKING AWAY 1

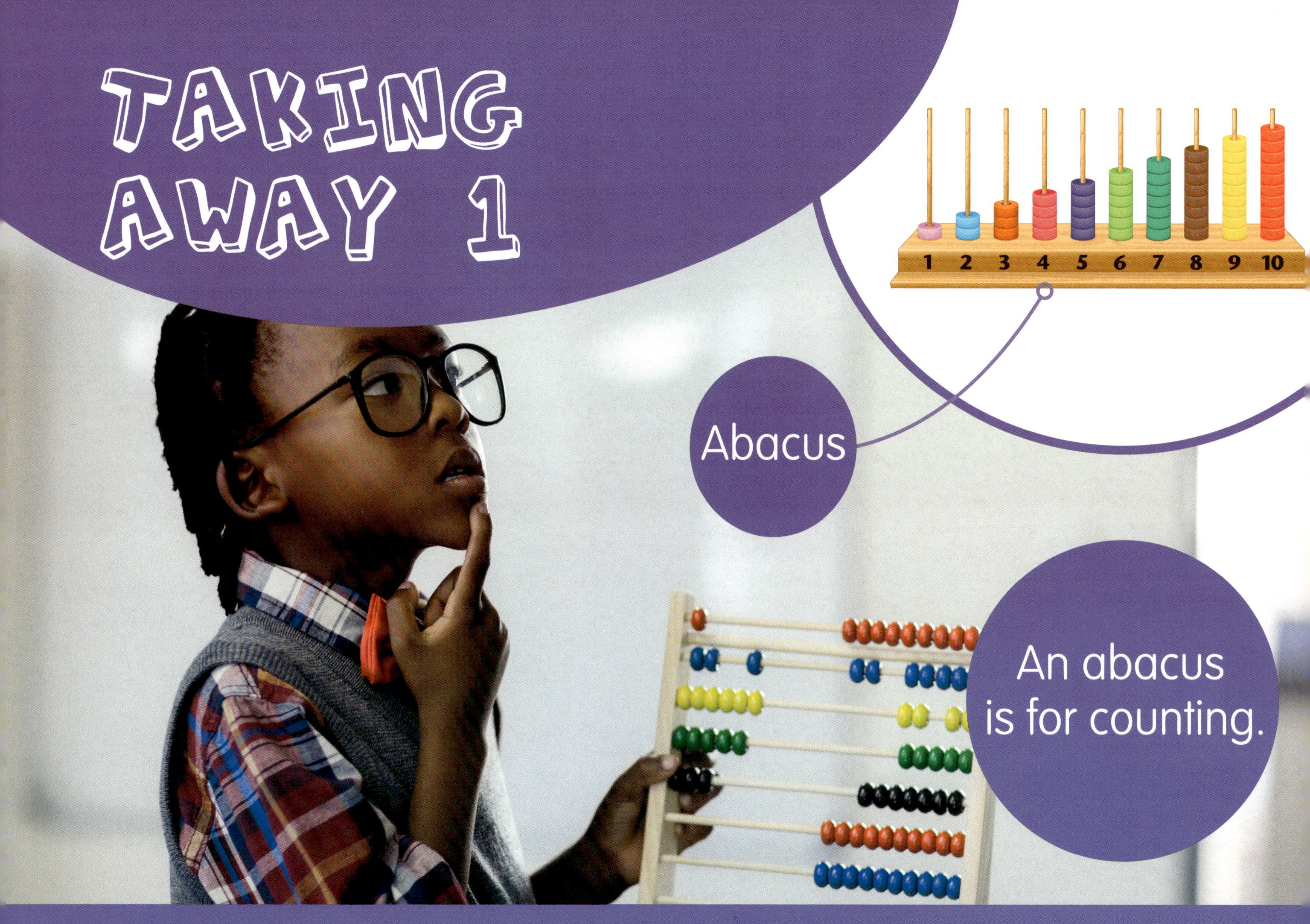

Abacus

An abacus is for counting.

When you count backwards, you are taking away 1 each time.

When you subtract beads, there are not as many left.

Each line has 1 less bead.

WHAT ARE – AND =?

These are all ways of saying subtract.

Minus

Subtract

Take away

If you see a line like this, it means take away.

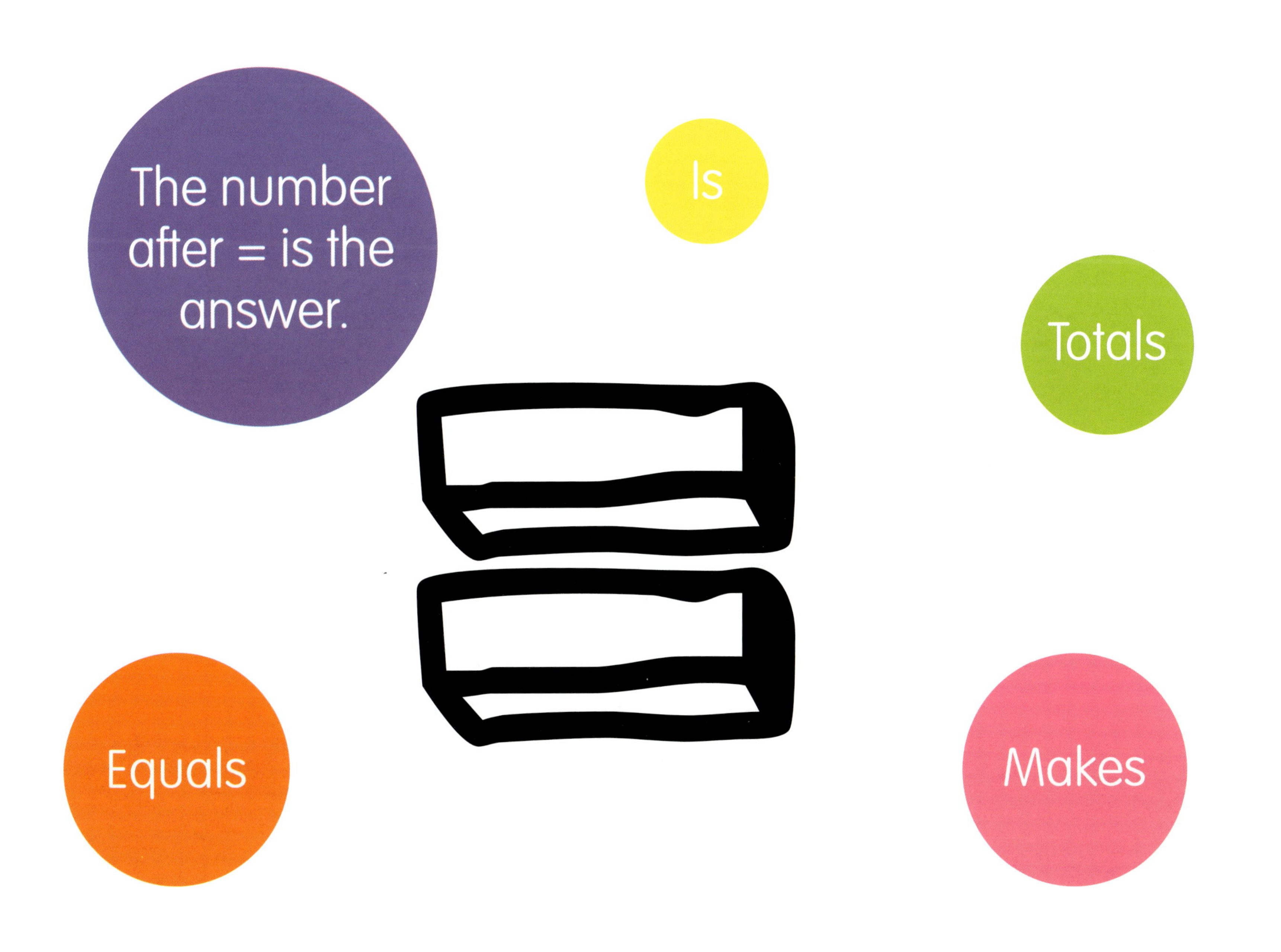

This is an equals sign.
It tells us what the answer is.

START SUBTRACTING

There are 5 flowers. We want to take away 1 flower.

There are 4 flowers left.

$5 - 1 = 4$.

TAKE AWAY TOYS

Here are 6 toys. Take 2 away.
How many are left?

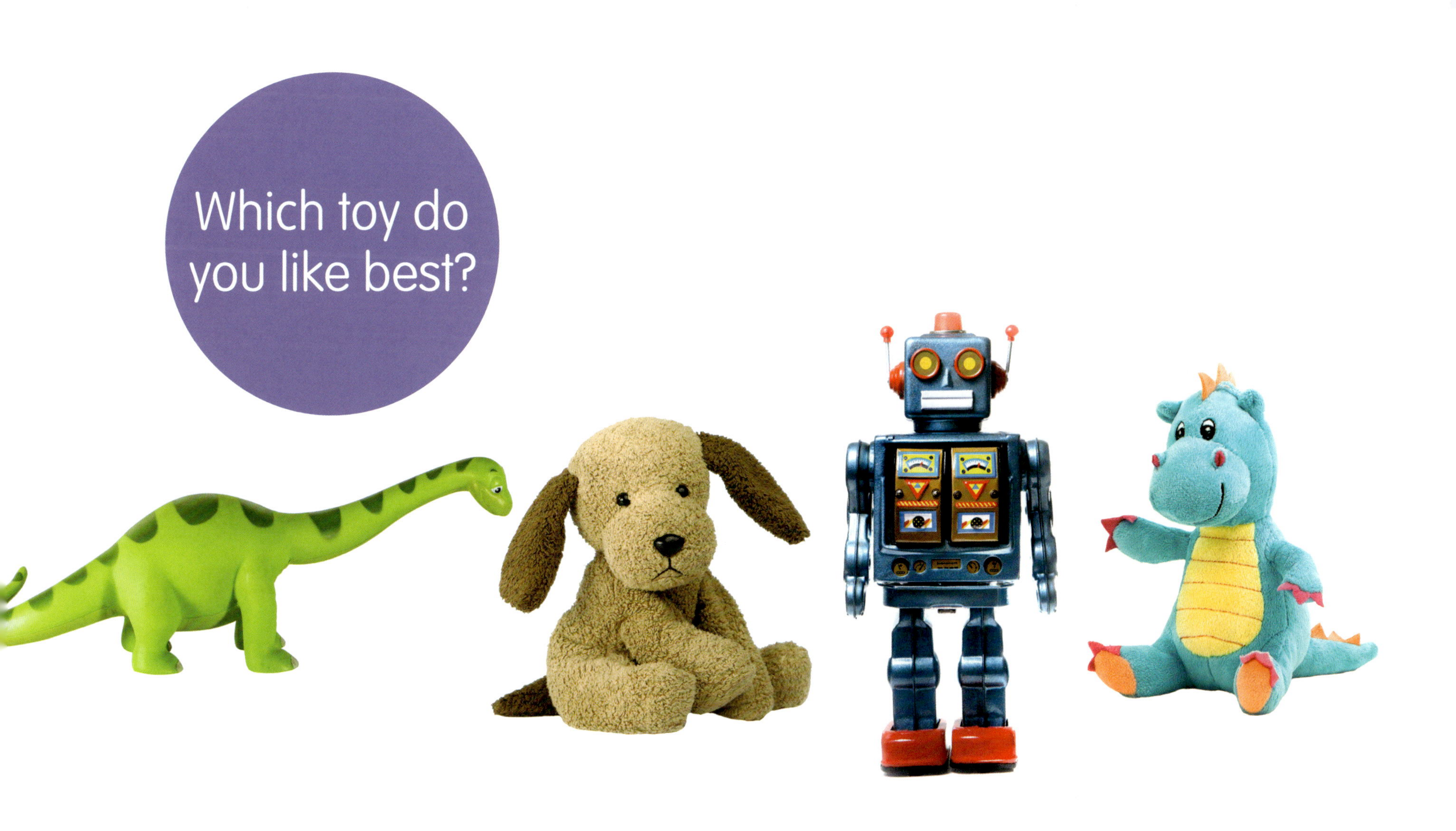

Which toy do you like best?

Did you count 4? 6 – 2 = 4.

SHARE YOUR CANDY

How many candies do you have left?

$6 - 3 = ?$

You have 6 candies. You give your friend 3 candies.

The answer is 3. 6 minus 3 equals 3.

SUBTRACTING FUN

How do we say this out loud?

They are both right!

HOW MANY?

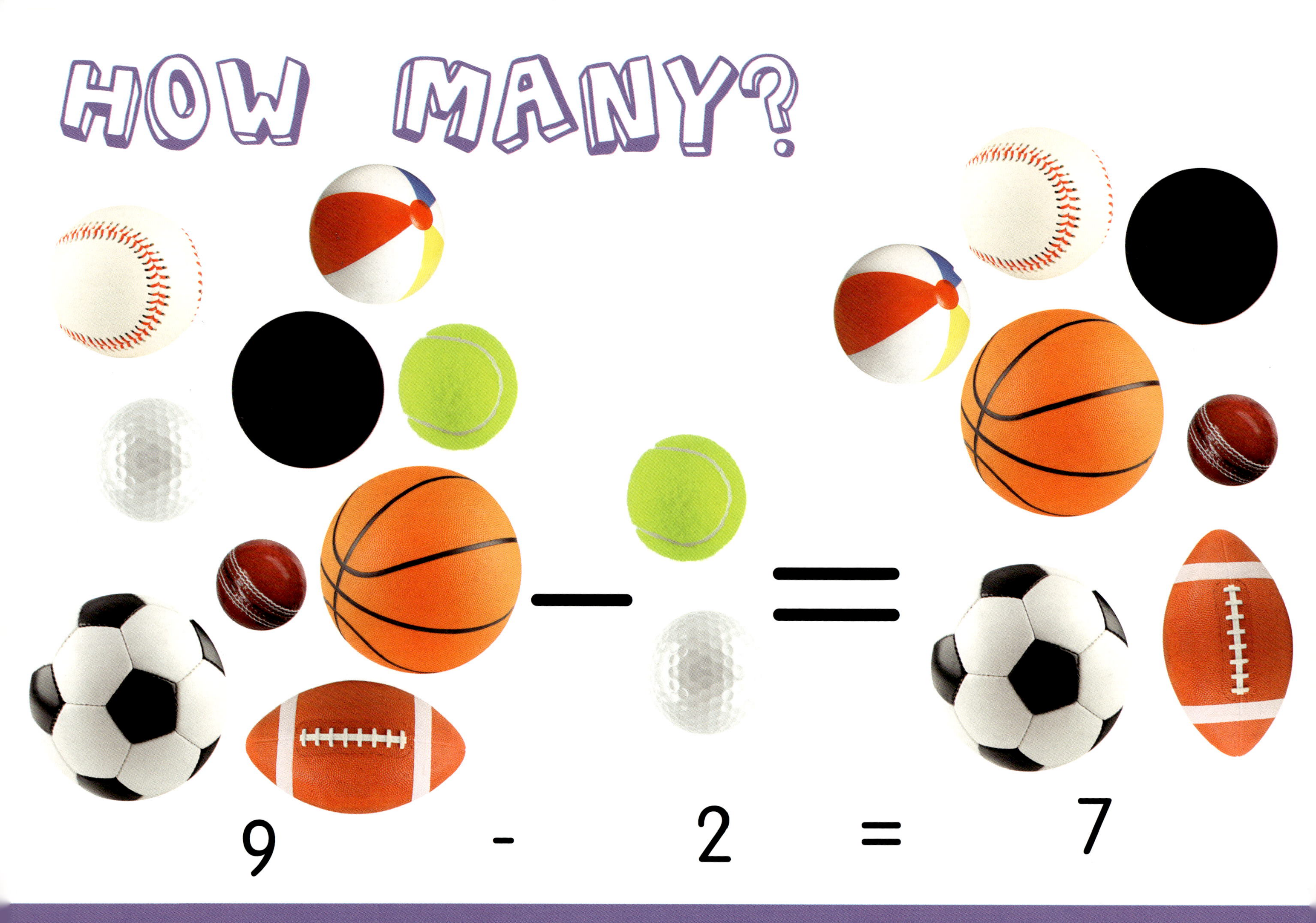

Count to find out how many are left.

You can use things to help you subtract.

SUBTRACTING NUMBERS

$8 - 3 =$ 

a) 7
b) 5
c) 2

Answer: b) 5

What number should go in the box?

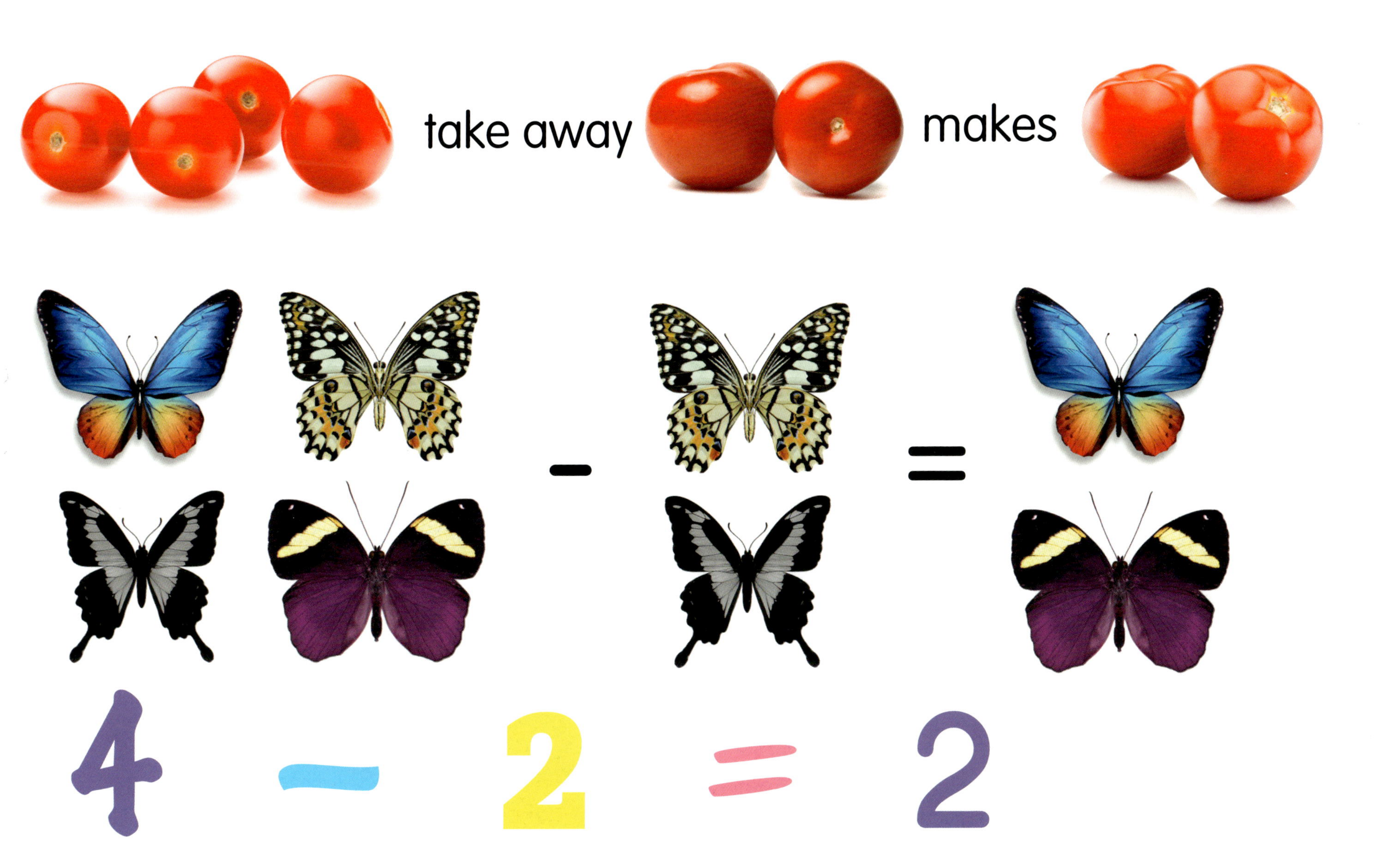

These all look different, but they all mean the same thing. You just have to take away.

FUN THINGS TO DO

Can you figure out how many have been taken?

Fill a tray with objects.
Close your eyes and have a friend take some away.